To Jeanne i Jeff

Looking forward

to more great parties!

Betsy i Sinda

Dec. 2006

P. S. Don't disappoint us.

20 PARTY TRICKS

To Amuse and Amaze Your Friends

20 PARTY TRICKS

TO AMUSE AND AMAZE YOUR FRIENDS

SOPHIE BLACKALL

CHRONICLE BOOKS

SAN FRANCISCO

Thanks to Leith Hillard for writing most of the book,
Sheringbone for design and layout, and Simon.

First published in the United States in 1997 by Chronicle Books.

Printed in Hong Kong.

ISBN: 0-8118-1659-1

Library of Congress Cataloging-in-Publication Data available.

Cover and text design: Elizabeth Van Itallie

Distributed in Canada by
Raincoast Books
8680 Cambie Street
Vancouver, B.C. V6P 6M9

10 9 8 7 6 5 4 3

Chronicle Books
85 Second Street
San Francisco, California 94105

www.chroniclebooks.com

CONTENTS

iNTRODUCTioN

Welcome to the world of party tricks. This is the little book which most people will keep hidden lest others learn the source of their Saturday night brilliance. You may wish to do the same!

In selecting these tricks we have tried to provide a cross section of opportunity for even the clumsiest of the clan. Mind you, not every trick is that easy and many are well-nigh impossible to perform successfully on a regular basis. However, all of them have been tested by the author and a little practice before performing them in front of an audience is strongly recommended.

Finally, a few words of caution. . . . Some of the tricks involve eggs; others require the use of matches or needles, all of which can cause harm to the exponent or audience. Please take care. Practice them before performing them. Always have a blank check at hand for offended or injured guests.

We take no responsibility for your fame or your misfortune.

HARMLESS TRICKS

PUTTiNG YOUR HEAD THROUGH A BUSiNESS CARD

Perhaps you're at a Very Important Party where people wear cult clothes and use secret handshakes; it's the subtle contact sport of networking in action. Hand the scissors to anyone who thinks they can cut the card in such a manner as to enable them to put their head through the center. Then watch them put their foot in it.

Here's how you can get ahead of the competition. . . . Fold the card the long way so that the two wide edges meet. Then cut a series of parallel slits from the fold to within ⅛ inch of the wide edges. Turn the card over, without unfolding it, and cut another series of slits in the opposite direction to, and between, the slits in the first series, from the wide edges to about ⅛ inch from the fold. Now cut along the fold, beginning at the first slit and being careful not to cut beyond the last slit. Unfold the card and gently pull the narrow edges away from each other. If you have enough slits you should be able to extend even a small business card sufficiently to put your head through the opening made.

This trick is also popularly known as "The Window of Opportunity." Enjoy the view.

FLoATiNG THE NEEDLE

Wise people say it is easier for a camel to fit into a glass of water than to make a needle float on top. Wiser people say it is easy to make a needle float, and park that camel outside, please.

Take a piece of thin paper, perhaps a cigarette paper or tissue paper, and float this on the surface of the water. Very carefully place the needle on top of this floating paper, making sure that no part of the needle touches the water.

Very gently push the corners of the paper under the water, without disturbing the position of the needle, then watch the result. The paper will slowly sink and leave behind it, floating on the surface, the needle.

Congratulations! Bottoms up and collect your bets, but not before that sharp little object is removed from the glass.

PiCKiNG TWo CoiNS OFF A GLASS

Sweat on the brow, sweat on the lip: face the challenge in this Olympian event requiring a Grand Chess Master's powers of concentration, great wrist action, and lithe and nimble fingers.

Balance two large coins opposite one another on the rim of a glass. Now challenge others to pick up both coins at the same time between only the thumb and index fingers of one hand. Bamboozlement all around is the result.

Step up and place your hand well above the glass, with the thumb above one coin and the index finger above the other. Hold the glass steady with your other hand. Lower thumb and finger until they are in contact with the coins, simultaneously tipping the coins over the outer sides of the glass, and hold them between the glass and your thumb and finger. Now quickly draw the coins along the glass toward you until they meet, when you will be able to pinch them together and remove them from the glass.

In the great tradition of legerdemain, now that you've pinched the picked coins, pocket them.

SLiPPERY CORKS

Perhaps, as a child, you had a beautiful toy ripped, untimely, from your arms, and handed down to your sister. Or you were ruler of the playground until your position was usurped by snotty Johnny Rotten. Have you always chosen the horse who came second; and was Buzz Aldrin your favorite astronaut on that historic mission? For all the losers and try-hards, this is one for you; the one that won't get away.

You'll need two wine corks of the same size. Stand them ends up on a table, side by side, touching each other, and ask if anyone present can lift the corks between the ends of the index and second fingers of one hand. The corks will roll away every time unless you bend your fingers slightly at both the first and second joints. In this way the corks can readily be picked up.

Walk tall. You'll wake up and tomorrow will be a bright, sunny day. You're a winner.

THE RISING PUSHPIN

Alexander the Great, Margaret Thatcher, Mussolini, kingpins all, worked their way relentlessly to the top, treading on heads and toes in their ruthless ambition, their steely eyes focused unwaveringly on that promised El Dorado. But now, from kingpin to pushpin . . .

Pour a glass of carbonated water; anything clear and fizzy will do. Drop a plastic pushpin into the glass where it will fall to the bottom. Mutter a bit of hocus-pocus, abracadabrize, do the hokey-pokey and turn yourself around. You'll find that the pin is doing all the work, but you'll be able to take the credit. Bubbles will form around the pin and force it to the surface, just as you have magically commanded.

Accept the fawning praise of your audience.

OFFENSIVE TRICKS

THE SEVERED FINGER

What this trick lacks in charm and sweetness it makes up for in shock value, enough to make die-hard smokers give up for life. It will also make you feel like a child again; approximately a five-year-old.

Cut a hole in the bottom of a matchbox large enough to insert your index finger. Whiten your finger with a little powder, draw on some bruises, dollop on a little ketchup and tuck into the box along with some cotton balls.

Close the box as far as you can. Hold it in the palm of your hand so people can't see that your finger is the one in the box. Look around for smokers who are about to light up and offer them a match. . . . Screams of enjoyment, howls of delight, squeals of laughter.

HANDY TIP: If you perform this crowd pleaser at your own party you may save a fortune on catering.

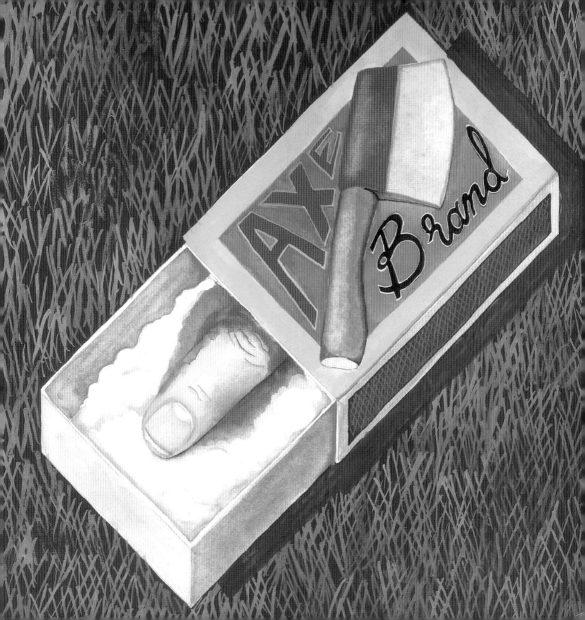

REPELLENT FINGER TRICK

As bees to ketchup; as the gutter press to a five-year-old's birthday party; like politicians to the genuine truth (and I really do mean that quite sincerely), so is the principle of the repellent finger trick. Marvel as the grains of pepper hightail it off into the sunset, as far away from your repulsive finger as an inanimate condiment can get.

To set the repulsion in action . . .

Fill a white bowl or dish with water, and scatter ground pepper on the surface. Any ignoramus who puts their unskilled finger in the bowl will see precisely nothing happen. Rant and rave a little, to give the water time to settle. Surreptitiously squeeze some liquid detergent onto the end of your finger, then plunge it into the bowl. Watch the pepper shoot to the edges and cower there in a dark ring, leaving the surface of the water immaculate.

You might think that you've discovered an alternative method of dishwashing with this trick, but the repulsive call has its limitations.

THE BROKEN ARM

We'd ask you to hold on to your hats for this one, but you'll find that you won't have enough extremities to go around. While you're still fully intact and capacitated, listen carefully to this particularly tricky trick.

Wear a long-sleeved shirt with the cuff down over the wrist. Drop your left arm at your side and hold the end of the sleeve between the fingers and palm. Place this forearm on the table, release the sleeve and extend the fingers, holding them together, knuckles under, palm up. With the right hand, strike the elbow joint of the left arm. Hold the left hand between the thumb and fingers of the right and pull it away from the sleeve. The arm will appear severed.

With the right hand lift the left to a position perpendicular to the table, keeping the left elbow in place. The right hand now bends the left down until it is parallel with the table, the forearm remaining perpendicular. Then, holding the back of the left hand between the thumb and fingers of the right, swing it in a half circle from left to right until it is pointing directly away from you.

Practice makes perfect, but don't imagine that perfect practice means actual arm lopping.

HYPNOTIC TOUCH

This trick will render your audience speechless, your victim helpless and you peerless. Choose, as your victim, someone who needs to be kept in their place. Show no mercy as you pin them in their chair with just the touch of your finger—well, perhaps just a little mercy, or they will display the same ruthless attitude as they pass their chiropractor's bills on to you.

Direct the piece of putty in your hands to a chair. Get him or her to fold their arms and extend their legs. Stand behind the chair and order them (nicely) to look up at you. Stand sufficiently far away so that, in order to see you, they must throw their head far back.

Place a finger on their forehead and say (or chant): "You cannot get up. You cannot get up," adding any other incantations that sound impressive. As long as you keep your finger on their forehead they cannot rise from the chair, because your finger prevents them moving their head forward.

How long does the trick last? A few minutes is plenty.

THE ERECT MATCH

What a proud and upstanding stunt this is. It positively thrusts itself into the lime-light with its forceful bearing and striking effectiveness. You'll be able to work the room or even the party circuit with this one. Ever onward and upward.

Take three matches and wedge two of the matches into the corners of one end of a closed matchbox. (The air is so thick with excitement and possibility, you could cut it with a knife. But, no: that's another trick altogether.) Bring the sulphur ends together so they meet in a point.

Place this arrangement on a saucer, and balance the third match on the edge of the saucer with the sulphur end touching and caressing the other two. (Tension is mount-ing, unbearably mounting.)

Light the three matches so that they flare up and join at the heads. As they burn down the third match rises up as if to greet the coming dawn. (Explosive finale complete with fireworks, seeing stars, wobbly knees.)

VITAL TIP: Remember to put the matches into the end of the matchbox away from the match heads.

MESSY TRICKS

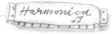

MUSICAL GLASSES

This is one of the easiest tricks to perform, but surprisingly few people know how. It is also the depth of bad manners at most dinner tables and caution is advised when displaying your newfound musical ability. If, however, you feel emboldened by the spirit of the occasion (and perhaps the quantity you have imbibed) and start up during the Governor's speech, don't despair. We know several people who make a satisfactory living playing wineglasses, although the venues are often windy. Anyway, this is how you do it . . .

Take a wineglass with a reasonable diameter, and pour in a splash of your favorite tipple. Swill this round a couple of times, then dip your index and forefingers into the liquid. Making sure that they are both wet, push firmly down on the rim of the glass and at the same time start slowly rotating your fingers around the rim. You may find that the initial moisture soon dries up, so you will need to dip your fingers into the wine glass again. Keep rotating them on the lip of the glass while maintaining the pressure, and in almost no time you will have found the lost chord.

N O T E : This trick is not recommended to be performed on expensive thin-stemmed champagne glasses unless you have already played at Carnegie Hall and know the strength of your fingers.

FLYiNG AMARETTi

The ace fighter pilot climbs into the cockpit of his gleaming machine. Oh, Great Flying Amaretti, we who are about to witness your acrobatics salute you. Though you are only a small Italian almond biscuit wrapped in tissue paper and available in quality delicatessens, we hail your bravado as you set off into the perilous beyond.

Here's how to send our hero on his way . . .

For optimum takeoff, the room must be free of wind (including the guests' hot air). Unwrap the amaretti and discard the biscuit—eat it if you have to. Smooth out the paper, roll it loosely into a cylinder and stand it on a plate.

Light the top rim of the cylinder, then sit back for the sky show. Signor Amaretti will rise into the air and float to the ceiling. When the flame dies he will return gently to your plate as a pile of ash.

Legend has it that the height reached by Flying Amaretti is a reflection of your love life: are you a lover or a fighter; soaring or nose-diving. The pilot of the heart will reveal all.

EXCHANGING WINE FOR WATER

What are the abundant loaves and fishes of the dinner party without a little lively accompaniment. So, while the crusts of the guests mop up the juices, clap hands and bring on the dancing horses. Here is a neat little trick straight from the New Testament.

Fill two matching wineglasses absolutely brimful, one with water and the other with red wine. Cover the glass of water with a piece of thin cardboard large enough to just cover the glass. Quickly turn the glass upside down while holding the cardboard in place, then release your hold on the cardboard. Place this glass and cardboard exactly on top of the other wineglass, so that both rims coincide at every point. Double check.

Now, slowly withdraw the cardboard from between the two glasses, so that close to $1/4$ inch is left between the edge of the cardboard and the rims of the glasses. Watch the water descend and the wine ascend. This will continue until they have fully exchanged glasses.

Is the wine making you see double? Is the water causing your vision to swim? No, this is a mysterious yet trouble-free exchange of fluids.

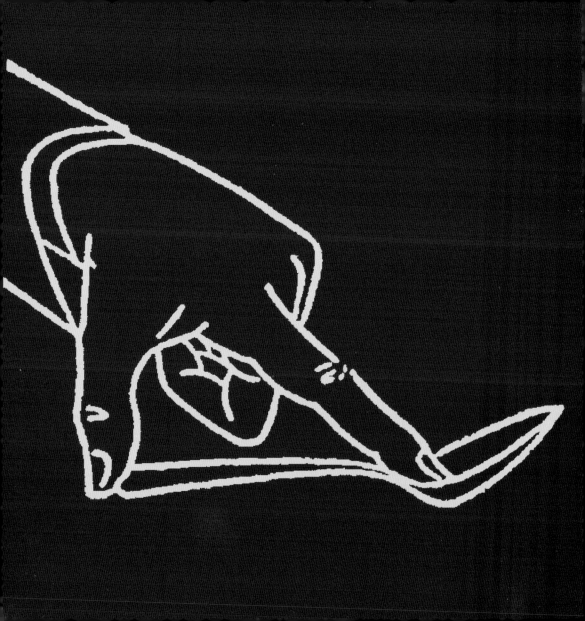

DIFFICULT TRICKS

MAGNETIC FINGERS

Our lives are but a quest: for the right partner, for meaning, and for the right hair-cut. For this attractive little stunt you must journey far for the right teaspoon. Not every teaspoon is ripe for the task, although spoons of other shapes and sizes can sometimes do the trick—or rather, you can do the trick with them. Experimentation will guarantee success; indifference may cause social exile in a sea of humiliation.

To lift a teaspoon off the table by putting the tip of your index finger in the bowl of the spoon and your thumb at the end of the handle, you must first magnetize your fingers. Rub your thumb and index fingertips vigorously on the tablecloth, then place your fingers on the spoon. Press the index finger down hard, then lightly pinch the handle, raising the spoon at the same time. You will certainly attract some admiring looks.

Experts can raise as many as four spoons simultaneously: the handles of all four touching the thumb, and the bowls of the spoons each in contact with a different finger. A career in television awaits you.

SPOON ON THE NOSE

Some people are born with a plastic spoon in their mouths; some are born with a blue ribbon emblazoned across their chests; most of us are born with a squashed and pointy head and ears that stick out at a hideous angle.

This crowd-pleasing feat will make you look quite the born-again clown; the original party-stopper born to wear a teaspoon attached to your nasal protuberance.

Just follow this simple step-by-step . . .

Breathe heavily and hotly into the bowl of a teaspoon, then place the bowl over the end of your nose. (Do not press it on too hard.) The teaspoon will now cling tenaciously to your nose for a short period.

Don't be too ambitious about holding the room for an hour with this one. But then again, perhaps you could work this act up into a full cutlery extravaganza, with a knife balanced on your tongue and a fork poised on each eyebrow. Not a trick to be sneezed at and certainly not one to be sneezed with. Facial disfigurement could ensue.

CHiCKEN TEA ToWEL

The versatility of the humble chicken truly knows no bounds. Dressed to kill in feather cloak, we have the creator of the egg, that staple of civilization. In its cluckless and plucked state, we have the tender thigh and breast, the treat for many a chicken lover living in a chicken shack out on the chicken run. Into this homely scene we bring the ultimate domesticated fowl; the chicken tea towel.

Present a lowly tea towel to the assorted company (preferably a fleshy pink one). Roll both ends of the tea towel into the center, then fold in half lengthwise and hold the four rolled ends in one hand. With the other hand, grasp each point within the rolls and tug.

Hold two opposite ends in each hand and pull open. If you pull the correct ends apart, you'll be able to keep one "pair of feet" in your hand and let the other drop. You'll be holding one large chicken (plucked cotton) in the hand, which is surely worth two in the wash.

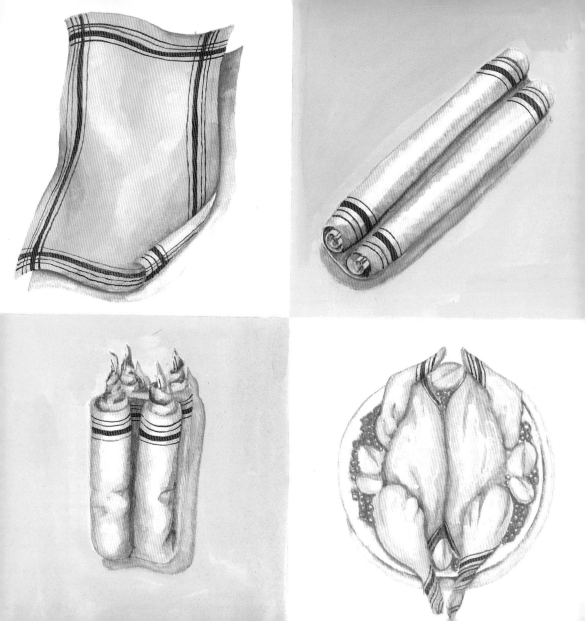

WATER iN THE PLATE

Wasn't it Salvador Dali who, in one of his moments of particular genius, passed on to us the image of a bicycle and some other piece of incongruous paraphernalia, in congress on an operating table?

This stunt also takes us down Nonsensicality Street, with its challenge to get the little water from a plate into a glass without moving the plate from the table, and assisted by fire and some money. The party guests might try paying the fire brigade to sort this one out. Here's how to outsmart them.

Cover the base of a plate with a small amount of water. Bend a match in half without breaking it apart. Place it in the center of the plate, held in place under the weight of a coin. Light the match and quickly place a glass over it. As the match burns, the water will be sucked up into the glass.

The party guests, too, will be sucked up into the vortex of this miraculous prank, along with the firemen, and carried away on a wind of pseudoscientific wonderment. Maybe.

PRE-SLICED BANANA

Carmen Miranda, that veritable fruit cocktail of a performer, was well known for shaking her booty. No shy, retiring Banana Mouskouri, this one; no crooner of pawpaw-pitiful-me ballads. This bold and brassy entertainer went where no other performer covered in a salad of plastic fruit pieces had ever gone before.

Razzmatazz. We want to take you back by showing you something show-stopping to do with a banana. Get a hat pin long enough to go all the way into the banana and still leave enough for you to hold on to. Prick the pin into the banana and work it from side to side, slicing all the way through the flesh of the fruit, but leaving the peel intact.

Pull out the pin and repeat for each slice. Ensure that you do this not long before the hapless monkey peels the banana, else your trick will be revealed by discoloration on the skin around the holes.

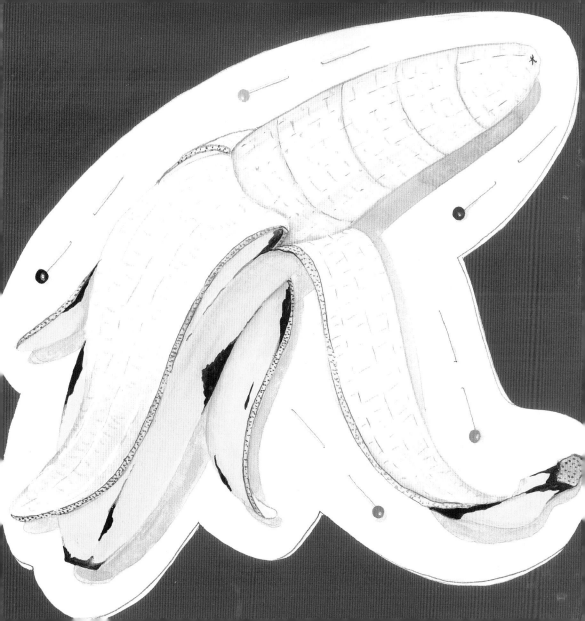

Bottling a Hard-Boiled Egg

Ah yes, many's the night we've sat around the fire warming the cockles of our hearts and toasting our health. We'd share a few stories of the old times, and reminisce about that-which-can-never-die-but-lives-on: The Pantheon of Egg Tricks.

Here's an oldie but a goodie. . . . Stand a shelled, recently hard-boiled egg on top of a milk bottle or similar bottle with a diameter of at least one inch, with the pointed end of the egg pointing down. Now ask if anyone can get the egg into the bottle without damaging either. Stun the assembled company with your skill. Drop a small piece of burning paper into the bottle, and replace the egg in the opening. Gasps of amazement. The egg will be sucked into the bottle without damage.

Getting the egg out is not so easy and requires practice if you want not to end up with egg on your face. Lift the bottle up over your head and blow into it with great gusto. Your huff should compress the air in the bottle sufficiently to force the egg out.

BALANCING THE EGG

Let's examine the egg. Never the bridesmaid and never the bride. Neither tinker nor tailor (but certainly omelette maker). The good egg is quiet. It knows its place. It's reliable and steady; a decent plodder never seen on the winner's podium, but then again, never lying on the therapist's couch. It's well adjusted; well balanced. We look at the egg and it says to us, "sanity, normality."

Here's an easy balancing trick. Pour a small pile of salt onto the table, and balance an egg in the middle of the pile. Blow the salt away, except for a few almost invisible grains that hold the egg in place, seemingly precariously.

Ummm . . . That's it . . . No fireworks. Just an egg trophy standing tall and proud, proclaiming, "I am."

THE END

SOPHIE BLACKALL is a colorful (and tricky) illustrator whose passions include watching *The Sound of Music*, discussing strange ailments, and practicing stain removal. She aspired to become Miss Almond Blossom 1977, but failed miserably. Instead, she began a long and difficult path through private schooling and turned her young talents toward the writing of a precocious play about Sister Mary MacKillop, Australia's first hope for a saint (Mary didn't make the cut), which was performed at many venues throughout the country. Some years later, in 1992, she graduated from the University of Technology, Sydney, with a degree in Visual Communication, receiving honors for her paintings on vintage cocktail trays that artfully juxtaposed lewd nursery rhymes with portrayals of the domestic joy of brides. Her work has since appeared in numerous magazines and gallery exhibits. She has traveled around Europe and China, but prefers to call Sydney, Australia, home.